Blues NARRATIVES

Sterling D. Plumpp

TIA CHUCHA PRESS
CHICAGO

ACKNOWLEDGMENTS
Nadia Swerdlow, who read the entire six hundred pages or so and suggested useful
morphological changes, Tricia O'Connor, who read the entire manuscript first and
encouraged the author with her supportive comments; Kimberley Ruffin and Deborah
Um'Rani, whose ears assured me that I had no problems with the female personae; and
Judy Belsky, who codones the manuscript and privileges its "universal statement."
Thanks.

Printed in the United States of America

ISBN 1-882688-20-1

Library of Congress Catalog Card Number: 99-72531

Book design: Jane Brunette

PUBLISHED BY: DISTRIBUTED BY:
Tia Chucha Press   Northwestern University Press
A project of the Guild Complex   Chicago Distribution Center
PO Box 476969   11030 South Langley Avenue
Chicago IL 60647   Chicago IL 60628

Tia Chucha Press is supported by the National Endowment for the Arts, the Illinois Arts
Council, City of Chicago Department of Cultural Affairs, The Chicago Community
Foundation, and the Lila Wallace-Reader's Digest Fund.

To Victor Emmanuel,
my maternal grandfather
and the only daddy I ever knew,
man of blues and prayers,
dance with the ancestors and rest,
then dance some more, Poppa.

Table of Contents

Mary (1920-1980): Dialogue With My Mother

Everybody
got laughter from sunrise
all day, every day
even the setting sun
tell you
Hi

Said everybody
got laughter from sunrise
all day, every day
even the setting sun
tell you
Hi

But I
got so much bad
luck even the day
breaks tell me

Goodbye
Goodbye

1.

I can under
stand you not
being concerned a
bout the formality
of a license

And I can under
stand you not
being immaculate

But I can
not under
stand why you did
not bring home

a carpenter

I get no
thing for living
not even a certified
cry

I get no
thing for living
not even a certified
cry

but I promised
a guaranteed pension
when I die

2.

Have
you ever been down
so low
you beg your hours
for a dime

Have
you ever been down
so low
you beg your hours
for a dime

Can't buy
a elevator ride
for your spirit
cause your days
doing time

Your breath
your eyes
and the good
byes in your touch
tell me
you are
boarding silence

and I do
not long
to march with you
on your journey

Not be
cause you were
only with me
long enough for
my umbilical
link to be

severed but not
long enough for
me not
to be introduced
to you years later
by your mother

I am partial
to the bad
times cause good
times won't let me
grow

I am partial
to the bad
times cause the good
times won't let me
grow

I plant
my deeds in uncertainty
where pain
opens a door

3.

I'm running, always running
through a concrete and
a steel wall

I'm running, always running
through a concrete and
a steel wall

I eat gunpowder
for my cereals
Wash it down
with bad alcohol

I apologize
for having
so much to say a
bout your death
since your days
left dictionaries
about your life

I would
not have had them
cut you

if I had thought
the cancer
would be pain
then gone

ache and
ebb policy

and not the lay a
way deal
over forty eight
months

Sitting here wondering
if I spent
my last penny
would I get back
any change

Sitting here wondering
if I spent
my last penny
would I get back
any change

Every step
I take is quicksand
Every turn
I make is a firing range

4.

I was raised
by evil and bad
luck in all their
many deeds

I was raised
by evil and bad
luck in all their
many deeds

Road a
head ain't got light
and my journey
bleeds

I am by
your bed
side not to hear
your moans

but to prevent
the nurse
who might wake you
up wrong
or IV you wrong

from being
whacked by you

But I want
you to know
that leaving a
child with grand
parents ain't
no crime

ain't no neglect

at all

I don't need
to tell you
it recorded in the days

I don't need
to tell you
it recorded in the days

I ain't blue
and I ain't sad
cause I lived my life
in all my many ways

5.

I take all my troubles
I stack them up on a shelf
I take all my troubles
I stack them up on a shelf

I am
a girl so blue and lonesome
I gotta carry my blues
all by myself

When the mid
wife carved me from
your fate
bound my reaches
for your mother

and I can remember
no cries
for your absences

I did
not though ever
want to know
your lovers
benign or cruel

I did
not though ever
want to know step
daddies or their up
bringings' expectations
of me

A male
child imagines
his mother

and you stole
part of my fantasy

I got
so many troubles
I send half to school
I got
so many troubles
I send half to school

Ain't much
else to do
when down and out
the golden rule

6.

I wonder
where will my children
get milk
cause my cow is skinny
and ain't got
no calf

I wonder
where will my children
get milk
cause my cow is skinny
and ain't got
no calf

They
can collect a bucket full
of tears and drink
Lawd till they laugh

So as I watch
you retreat from
laughter that signifies
joy and shouts
and devilment
you grow in
side affirmations
of long rainy nights

evil knife
toting cotton
bolls and open fields
of longings
you follow

I long for stories
I know as you

Railroad crossing
Railroad crossing

Place I always at
when it rains

Railroad crossing
Railroad crossing

Place I always at
when it rains

My dreams
can't jump on
but off jump a thousand
hoboing pains

7.

Daybreak wakes
my pains in the morning
Sunset reads
to my hurts
at night

Daybreak wakes
my pains in the morning
Sunset reads
to my hurts
at night

Worry
Worry

all the time
no matter
if it's in the dark
or in the light

I got
this liberated anger
under house
arrest in my songs

And I know
it is no "Magnificat"

a black girl sings a
cross Mississippi hills
mud and red
clay choruses
throbbing with blisters

hoes dish
water and low
down men bring

And I can
not say a rosary
for you since
the only beads
you know

are knots
side your head
and columned
on your spirit

My dreams
just little birds
jumping from trees
to die

My dreams
just little birds
jumping from trees
to die

Got
no pretty colored
feathers on their wings
to make them fit
to fly

8.

I born
with snake
eyes and low cards
holding hands

I born
with snake
eyes and low cards
holding hands

Ain't got no
place to hide
cause chance gives me commands

There is no
where on this earth
or any
place else   Are

we put here
to mourn

hue men and hue
women, draw

laughter from
desires as
tourniquets for
losses they heal

every day
every day
every day

the wounds
they doctor
Lord, with words
they don't have
words for

My blues so low
down make me
sleep out of doors

My blues so low
down make me
sleep out of doors

Bricks and stones
my pillow
tomorrows draining out my pores

9.

I ain't a bad girl,
I just
take your broken week
ends/carry them home

Said I ain't a bad girl,
I just
take your broken week
ends/carry them home

Pull you
in my arms/roll you
till a month is gone

I can
not light candles
for you
because I know
you drank the last one
in your laughter
in your eyes

as you cut some
body with looks

The epoch between
the time
the white
woman you worked for
asked if it was all
right to come see
you and the millenium
when I replied yes

affirms the faith
I have in the medicine
of your travellings

I never
had no freedom
never had a day
without pain
never had nothing
but feeling bad
I never
had no freedom
never had a day
without pain
never had nothing
but feeling bad

I am so glad
the blues is all
I ever had

10.

My history is a school day
after goodtimes been let out
My history is a school day
after goodtimes been let out

I am all
alone in a vacant building
where I do with little
and Lawd I do without

I got a muzzle
for voices of
the ragged wind
crying Saturday
nights in
to my pewed laughter

And I got
this muted longing

I long
distances of floods
I cry
for you silently
ambivalent with
out regrets be

cause this calligraphy
of blood sculptured
by brother
and sister put
down rain

from days you
made in
side time hours in
debted you to

It is hard
I tell you
it is hard
to dance on a barrel
in a straight line

It is hard
I tell you
it's hard
to dance on a barrel
in a straight line

When a cotton
sack is my prom
dress and salty
sweat my glass
of wine

11.

*I call
my Lawd some
times/let go
a little of my mind*

*I call
my Lawd some
times/let go
a little of mind*

*Wanna
know if white folks
in heaven
Wanna
know if they color
blind*

You were never
evicted until
silence came
with a warrant

but your children
were/I was
at school
and Katie
Mae in bed
with the flu
The she
riffs sat
them both out
of the chords

and you return
a year later with
out a melody
or rhythm to handle
the puzzles

A son
and a daughter
fight for breathing
spaces in the epics
of your odd foot
steps

I am poor
blue and alone
on this long
road and

No
body
No
body

seems to care

I am poor
blue and alone
on this long
road and

No
body
No
body

seems to care

Got
a half day
on my back
Gotta
walk up a whole mile
on a broken
stair

12.

My
daddy call me
crying: what in the world
going on

My
daddy call me
crying: what in the world
going on

I say, baby,
more than one rooster
tickling my feathers
in the chicken yard
I
don't see what I am
doing wrong

I accept
you and I
love you though

you are an
invention a
bout origins

after I had
invented your
mother and my own
secret cosmology

You are an
other star
in an
other galaxy

I got
a call on the phone
and a voice asked
if I had American Express
or Visa/or could I
remit a payment any
other way

I got
a call on the phone
and a voice asked
if I had American Express
or Visa/or could I
remit a payment any
other way

Said it was
from heaven and I
needed to pay now
to guarantee twenty
four hours
in my day

13.

I moan
my song and
I do
not moan it
loud

I moan
my song and
I do
not moan it
loud

Cause
I am just a stranger
whether I am
all alone
or in a crowd

I commit
to memory your agony
and confessions of
the last slave to die
in America

(It is your responsibility
to carry it)

You tell

it to me hours before
you are gone

You pay my fare
wells with a request

The irony
you telling a son
stranded on a bridge

between love and ambivalence how

to assist you on
to the stage of exit

but the morgue
cosmetician thinks
you are going
to a party

I order him
to remove powder
and rouge
so blues
lines can still
reside in this symphony
of night which is
your face

When I
ask for bread
ask for medicine
ask for clothes
ask for rent

When I
ask for bread
ask for medicine
ask for clothes
ask for rent

They say
yesterday
that money was all
ready spent

14.

I
ain't got much
to say bout life
ain't got much
to say bout
being in love

I
ain't got much
to say bout life
ain't got much
to say bout
being in love

I know
I feel my journey
heading toward
somebody up
above

For years I
thought Santa
Claus would bring
you and my daddy
down the chimney

For years I
dreamed another
existence with parents

But like you I
find dampness
in parched lips
of desire and
my songs thrive

I believe my
self in
to a singer bound
in willingness

to trade pain
for metaphors
and lines
and stanzas

that owe
their styles
to your tale

your out
rageous wit
and longings
which disappear
when your voice
goes back to memory

and I search
the geography
of your days
to retrieve it

What
you gonna do
children, when you
wake without a future
What
you gonna do
children, when you walk
into a ought

What
you gonna do
children, when you
wake without a future

What
you gonna do
children, when you walk
into a ought

Make your
self a dream world
from one mighty dream
thought

15.

I find myself
with my blues
Lawd and I sure
don't understand

I find myself
with my blues
Lawd and I sure
don't understand

I cry
so hard
till I swear
that ain't no
such thing
as dry land

For you are
a memoir
crying in
to my pen

breathing tears
I shadow
box my
self to sleep
with

The Pilgrimage
to the hole
is brief
I will
not take flowers
from you since
petals of your dreams
and memories

are sequestered with
in my senses

And yes

a lady
wins the Derby
for you
and I remember hard
times you race

as echoes of
your laughter in
side my moans
have their way

> *Seems*
> *like I am heading*
> *down a one way rail*
> *road track*
>
> *Seems*
> *like I am heading*
> *down a one way rail*
> *road track*
>
> *I swear*
> *the past ahead*
> *and the future*
> *at my back*

16.

Once
I had spring
in my steps
Yes and bounce
in my thighs

Once
I had spring
in my steps
Yes and bounce
in my thighs

I
had a pad
lock on men's pocket
books and
a magnet on
their eyes

Remembrance of
your screams gets me
accommodations at
the Inn
of Rain
Forests in
side beliefs

you tilt air
with and I
tumble from up
stairs and

shout

These acryllic night
mares you paint on horizons
of my journey
I pursue

You
know Poppa
he had no
thing and
he passed it
on to me
when I was born

You
know Poppa
he had no
thing and
he passed it
on to me
when I was born

I am
so glad I got no
thing it gone be
here when I am
dead and
gone

17.

I
hit my road
sick in pain
or full of joy all
ways with a
smile

I
hit my road
sick in pain
or full of joy all
ways with a
smile

Tell
my Lawd for every inch
he give me
I
will definitely
walk another
mile

My consciousness
is a small
canvass where you
evaporate celebrations of
joy despite red
clay justice
and shot
gunned avarice

And startled
I be
gin mapping shadows
dressed in head
rags and aprons

I am kin
to hurts
pains and bad
troubles is
a first cousin
of mine

I am kin
to hurts
pains and bad
troubles is
a first cousin
of mine

I
got short
breath cause
the rest of it
my hard
times fine

18.

I
sit by the window
and dream
the roads
I have been

I
sit by the window
and dream
the roads
I have been

It
the main feature
of my being
I
watch over and over a
gain

I can
tell you no
body talked
too long
praising or
lamenting and
you were out

of sight on the out
skirts of immortality

when folks
gathered

My
road come
to a bend with
out a border
or sky

My
road come
to a bend with
out a border
or sky

I
believe I will
be allowed over
to the mansion
on high

19.

I
have live
my life
and the living
of three or
four

Said
I
done live
my life
and the living
of three
or four

As long as
I breathe
I long living
some more

Innocence is a
stranger not
an alien in
falling leaf

lets of your days
I know

where the open
door policy of
idle productivity

mortgages smiles
from thorns

and I stand
hoping that

the tonic bolts
of your lightning

bugs will shed
a little healing

on me

I/am so poor
ain't even
got a match
box or a purse

I/am so poor
ain't even
got a match
box or a purse

But where
I/am going
you know my suit
case will be
the universe

Victor (1880-1955)

1. SONG

Ah, boy/either
you a man or
you ain't

but when you
straddle the fence
I don't know whether
you trying to
stand up be
a man or trying
crawl back down
on the floor be
a baby again

Never had much
just my man
hood/my family
and my church
and my God
I fix up a place
for in my heart

Ah, boy you gotta
work at standing up
gotta learn how
find the prayer down in
side   but you all
ways straddling
the fence or you all
ways near it

All
you own are stained
glass windows
in silences   Where
there are no pews   There
are no altars   There are
no sanctuaries.

You all
ways said
when you wanted me
fight for my song
and search for
ways to say it

2. I AM DOOMED

But I
was told that
the hump

on your back
was your ornery
knoll where
you kept

your manhood

and the devil's
snuff you dip
when somebody
touch you

Then
I saw you
hind the cedars
patching a cloud
you hold

and when
you stand up
it sounds
like a earth
quake and tornado
talking the same
time and boxing
the air

then I know

it is your world
you carry
and I hear
you cry something
and look up

I know
I am doomed

Because your cry
tells me
what I see
is forbidden

tell me: ain't
no world without
the word

and I done seen
and heard yours

I am doomed

3. OLD SEAL

You
want me

because I saw

the stuttering
beatitudes of the North
Star pitch a wang
dang doodle in your left
eye where the blues

nothing but wild cherries

picked from vines
pain grows
from blood stolen
from a dream's heart

You
want me

and hooves of
Old Seal

the plow
horse find my face

because I will remember
because I will tell

You
want me
dead

because I will tell

I can
not drown
or swim in the distance
between us

so I turn
and run

and you
on Old Seal's shoulders
find my shadow and
push it through my thin
body

Yet
when she rears
to stomp down some
thing inside your hands
entices the reins
to have mercy and I open
my eyes to see your

back swaying against
the morning sun
and Old Seal trotting away

heading across
the wild fields
where I am sure

you cultivate
your dreams

We
remain adversaries
until your breath
stops on that Saturday
morning

when
we stare in
one another's
eyes and communicate
with silence

We
do not mend
fences

You
took me as
your son

because I will remember

I
know you and
I know I
was always memorizing
your agonies

calculating costs of
each of your steps
in Mississippi

I can
tell the price of
your breathing

because I know
there ain't no
world without
the word

because I remember
because I tell

Poppa
I can never
call you grand
daddy or grand
father because

you
is my Poppa
my big hands
my eyes to stare
at troubles
my feet
to challenge storms

You know
and I
know I

will tell your secrets

I will
tell your world
I will
tell your word

From your back
yard I read eye
lids of centuries

where America's history
is remediation with
out your blues
your world and
your word

4. BLUES NOT GONNA HIDE

Broken nausea of
spinning around and
around settles

deep in your hand
claps pleading
directions to

where I get my naming
license and gotta
erect doors in mud
corridors where you anoint
spaces that hide
clues to openings

in mud where you
planted them

with prayers that have
no borders between
holiness and blues

Blues
the round about
trail to God's ears
in ragged clothes
run down shoes
and bloody news smeared
on its sleeves

Your blues say
it not gonna hide its face
cause somebody bothered
by its presence
not gonna change its style
cause somebody shamed
by its contours
not gonna cut off its tone

cause somebody don't
wanna hear life crying
not gonna commit suicide
cause somebody can't
stand heat in my chords

My past is a cold
cold wind dressed
in a negligee
whose fingers
scrape my name

because time is handless
and I can
not reset its clock

I am a citizen of chaos
I patchwork
my angles of vision
from how I tell
and tell and tell
my days

some say I am illegitimate
they lie

I am a bastard
there is no legitimacy
in this land
for a skin
like mine where songs
are not mandatory

and where your patched
overalls and Momma's apron
and Little Black Angie's head
rag

the only kente cloths
I know

5. SPACE

Death
an alternating phrase
in a song remembered
and remembered

6. OPENINGS

You are a space
you say
between walls
in cracks where you can
grab hold of slavery's
chains and freedom's
slippery palms some
times

You are born
when they lynch and
lynch you say

You learn to count
screams of thousands
burning at stakes
ears chopped off
as souvenirs

Your blues you say
lead these screams
to heaven's door

They brought them
to me   the gravediggers
did   these silhouettes of
your memory

said they would
not stay buried

And I
hide them forty-one years
till now when I will
make a window from them

History is not
a river
where requests to the DJ
will bribe the Ferry
Man/such toll fees
are ineffective

They do
not erect bridges over
dry bones and exile

I
rise from your Papa-ganda
a son of furrows and time

My story
is the story of telling
and telling and telling and
telling

You
till and tell
like Malombo

use crude implements

to call spirits
to improvise paths

then tell me
I must get-tar
for roofs of my songs

and I get Buddy Guy

because to get
to your songs
ain't but two lines
running

one at midnight
the other just before
the break of day

I
take the matrilineal
line

and all
I see is a door with
out a key
hole or key

I tell you
I am working still

Parts of your tale
arranged in my mind
like furniture

How
you got the world
on your back
the living room

You are born to seas

and take me there
but I do
not have even
a ship made of paper

7. WAITING ON BREATH

But I remember

You almost
killed your nephew
the one that came to pick
up Bro your eldest son
at midnight that time
they said Bro was
a accomplice cause he help
Miss Willie Mae's boy
TP move some things

Your gun did
not know no law
and was about to shout
in the faces there
to take your boy away

then one of them said: Uncle
you kin go with us
we just sent to git him
not to beat him
and your gun
relaxed its stance
in your hands

I keep that night
in my eyes forty one
years and I saw it
grow dim in yours
in 1954

as you lay there
looking at the dreams
you cultivated even
in hills of the ceiling

You never leave
the bed voluntarily again

and your Mason brothers
would sit with you
keep away flies and
keep anybody from
learning your tale

I had it
and made sporadic
visits within your reach

cause I did
not know if sickness
could stop you
from waving some blade
against my flesh

But you remain
wordless and still
while we wait on you
and wait

My world
comes apart like shucks
unravelled from an ear of corn

and places that whispered songs
fourteen years called
my name less
and tattered edges of its sky
your calling on your Lord
stitched come loose

Your
breathing is the electric line
to my senses and it
is on the ground while
I wonder if there are
portable generators
to power my clarity

8. HALF OF EVERYTHING

You
slap your oldest child
down even though she
is forty because
she steps on your tale
under your roof and
you do not allow white
folks to enter your gate
or fields where your
children are working
because they might trample
on your tale

I understand

I watch you day
after day after
day eloquent even
in silence and in your
profile against a
lamp-lit room

Here
rivers of
your prayers echo
throughout the house
pivot on the ceiling
and dance over walls

Open
your mouth and Nobody Knows
the Troubles I See
takes its recess in tributaries of
wrinkles designing your features
The slave castle and middle
passage and auction block
are sculpted by tiers of
your blues falling

Lord falling
falling falling
like black night

I will tell

You go just before
the break of day
the time you would rise
for prayer before
journeys to the fields

I tell words from
your orations in a song
and some wise critic
say I get them
from Robert Johnson

My mind is a ramshacked house
I can not even find my name
Like an orphaned leaf
I float around edges
with no tree to anchor me
and no land to come down to
without a penalty

I sing
from darkness and
jumbled places

I remember
I tell

And the Boss Man
and the law come

ask if you told
your grandchilluns anything

said the agreement
said they git half
of everything: sayings
or tales
or things sketched
said if they find out
anytime they heirs
entitled to their halves
of your offspring
even curses or
prayers

Home
is where your tales
rise from are connected
to spaces and places
with flowers over door
ways and alleys

Home
is your fate
stunted body and awkward
gait with a spinning
world on your back

Home
is where your memory
and my voice consult
on battlefields of
vision our days offer

8. CALLING YOU BACK

Now
forty-one years
after you have been
only in memory
I see the old man
in your final pose
in my face and
I am eighteen years
away from the point
when you went into silence

I
call you sometimes
through seasons
where a daughter and
pages of poems represent
the memory from you
I weave sketches of
my existence on

I
call you sometimes
to lean on
when the tapestry of
my hours are indecipherable
and I need a voice
to re-invent passion
for toiling in fields
of the spirit
where there are
no calendars
there are no maps
and I must journey
and journey to survive

to remain the song
paving roads of memory
and creation

I invent and
re-invent and
re-invent

Always
trying to remove
my name from the grafitti of
nobodies society scribbles
on its centuries and
I escape
but return
like Tubman
with my songs and
dreams to find another world
inside fabrics of
this one

I
pile and pile my laughter
over chasms
so desires cross
over till they reach Armstrong
or Masuka carrying
lullabyes of generations
home in rhythms
that heal loneliness

I
have known all
alone that I must find
all your shadows
that ever danced
to know my soul

to get it from dreamless
torches worshipping
incarcerates it
in

I
have known all
alone

I
must recreate nuances
that service my imagination

9. SONG

*Ah, boy I don't
know meaning of death
or meaning of being
gone/All I know
the roads I travel
the places I stake
out my man
hood and fight
for my balls
The silence I don't
fear/the stillness
I don't fear/But
I wonder how long
the road of being
gone/Ah, boy
you vex me/but I
leave the length
of my roads/Fight
for it/and get off
the fence*

I think I hear
you but you gone
I think I see
you but you gone
I think I can
reach out touch
your short breath
but ain't no short
breath in death

and the road I
long grow longer
by the minute

A F T E R W O R D
Sterling Plumpp's Poetry

JOHN EDGAR WIDEMAN

*I*N STERLING PLUMPP'S poetry, what's astounding is the metaphorical and spiritual and material omnipresence of blues. Blues men and women and songs and themes and attitudes as ways of figuring, modeling, explaining a reality the poetry seeks to communicate. Another level of effort to wring from blues, to paraphrase, analyze, fuss, contradict, engage in dialogue with the messages blues contains, a philosophic inquiry about blues as world view, as consolation and rumination, long quarrel and reconciliation with godhead, blues as path for coming to terms with existence. Third, blues forms, language, rhythms translated, paralleled, suggested through the rhetorical and structural techniques of poetry — poetry & blues — to what degree are they permeable, transposable, welcoming — line length, line breaks, stanzaic patterns, refrains, tag lines, spacing (silence), rhyme, repetition, direct address, the bardic "I," the mimicking or indirect discourse of blues voices — singers, street people, musicians, family — melisma, slurring, call and response choral effects. Inventive analogues for characteristic blues devices such as the repeated, cumulative intensity of a blues "shout," an unchanging word or line or figure opening every line of a poem. The highly subjective, personal focus on telling one's story — directly, simply — so it stands for, invites, the collective drama as echo, affirmation. Can I hear somebody say, Amen.

And that's just a start, a bare bones on three levels of how blues saturates Sterling Plumpp's work. As astounding as the immersion in blues is the formidable sense of self. Whether in Mississippi or Capetown, the poet knows exactly who he is, writes with profound certainty of his roots. Not that he uncritically approves or romanticizes. Or brags. Or is blasé. Just knows where he came from. What conspired culturally, historically, politically, and at home to produce him, his concerns, his pain, his desires, his need to sing about it all. A paradox — part of what he knows so well about himself is of course the blues — and the blues are mysterious, irreducible, eternally open-ended, Promethean, in-progress, questions not answers, subject to change, alchemize, decay, despair, destabilize, transcend, get lost in the shuffle, overcome. So you don't get the sense the poet knows what's coming next, nor that the past is pat, a done deal. Rather, an ongoing sense of tension. The mode is discovery. What will work out. We know a lot, some of it we already foretaste — the 4/4 time, couplets, gravelly gut-bucket register, falsetto shriek, field holler, anticipate the rhyme or the familiar formulaic line from the traditional repertoire — but what they will make this time, where they will take us, is held back; we're in suspense, suspended in the medium. We won't know there till we go there. Three other qualities separate Plumpp, distinguish him: his degree of focus — intense, compressed, the blues a sort of navel or blade of grass he gazes at to see the entire universe; his discipline — which contains his ambitious project within the single tradition, the idiom of African American musical style; and his variety — in spite of his intense concentration and focus, he manages to range widely, he achieves, like the blues, an amazing outreach, capaciousness of tone, subject matter, form, scene, voice, within his chosen realm. Plumpp makes me feel the tenacity of his spirit's questing, the single-minded pursuit, the unrelenting importance and urgency he projects about the task of identifying, locating, then squeezing truth, art, from his blues roots. These poems dedicated or addressed to family members are signs of generosity, of a pervasive desire to show gratitude and to share. Poems are a means of saying thanks, of returning bounty for bounty, replenishing the source, the tradition. I'm grateful for the gift — beguiled, intrigued, enlightened. Finally, and maybe most important, his poems make me want to write.